✳✳✳✳✳✳✳✳✳✳✳✳✳✳✳✳✳✳✳✳✳✳✳✳✳✳✳✳✳✳✳✳✳✳

SPICE COOKERY

✳✳✳✳✳✳✳✳✳✳✳✳✳✳✳✳✳✳✳✳✳✳✳✳✳✳✳✳✳✳✳✳✳✳

✳✳✳✳✳✳✳✳✳✳✳✳✳✳✳✳✳✳✳✳✳✳✳✳✳✳✳✳✳✳

SPICE COOKERY

By

HELMUT RIPPERGER

He that hath spice may
season as he list.
Old English Proverb

COACHWHIP PUBLICATIONS
Greenville, Ohio

✳✳✳✳✳✳✳✳✳✳✳✳✳✳✳✳✳✳✳✳✳✳✳✳✳✳✳✳✳✳

Spice Cookery, by Helmut Ripperger
© 2018 Coachwhip Publications

Published 1942.
No claims made on public domain material.

CoachwhipBooks.com

ISBN 1-61646-450-X
ISBN-13 978-1-61646-450-9

* *

FOR

M. C. S.

WHO

IS THE SPICE

OF LIFE

* *

✻✻✻✻✻✻✻✻✻✻✻✻✻✻✻✻✻✻✻✻✻✻✻✻✻✻✻✻✻✻

FOREWORD

We read in the Book of Genesis that as soon as the sons of Jacob had carried out their plot against their brother Joseph, they sat down to eat; and lifting up their eyes, "behold a company of Ishmaelites came from Gilead with their camels bearing spicery and balm and myrrh, going to carry it down to Egypt." And so it was some seventeen hundred years before the Christian era that we find the Arabs in control of the spice industry, a control that Arabia Felix was to maintain until the sixteenth century and the discovery of a new passage to the Cape of Good Hope. The spice monopoly passed from the Portuguese to the Dutch and then, finally, to the English. And today, in the Year of Our Lord 1942, the English are re-importing their spices from the United States!

As I look upon my spice shelf and see the row of little bottles, Saigon Cinnamon, Tellichery Black Pepper, Amboyna Cloves, Jamaica Ginger, Banda Mace, and Sarawak White Pepper, to mention but a few, the radio in the next room announces the fall of Singapore. And it was only yesterday that

✻✻✻✻✻✻✻✻✻✻✻✻✻✻✻✻✻✻✻✻✻✻✻✻✻✻✻✻✻✻

SPICE COOKERY

❋ ❋

I read of the fighting in Amboyna. What if shipments from the spice islands were delayed, cut off temporarily or even entirely?

The United States Government announced recently that, if necessary, every known spice, herb, and seed could be grown in this hemisphere of ours. Cinnamon and cloves are being grown experimentally in Puerto Rico. The Greenbelt Government Station in Maryland is producing sage at the present moment. Some ten years ago, farmers in the Southwest began growing mustard seed. Looked upon then as being foolhardy, now, with no imports from abroad, they have produced more mustard than we ever imported. In the Ozarks and in Arkansas marjoram and sage as well are being grown. Caraway, which used to come from Holland and Germany, is now raised in Kentucky and Iowa. Paprika, long shut off from Hungary but which reached us from Spain and other sources, is being produced in California and it is also being cultivated in Mexico from Spanish seed. Nutmeg and mace, important spices from the Indies, come to us from the British West Indies. Ginger comes from Jamaica and India as well as from the far east. Coriander is coming from South America rather than from Europe and Morocco, and saffron from Mexico instead of the Mediterranean. Louisiana red pepper and cayenne are constantly growing in demand and popularity

❋ ❋

❀ ❀

now that the African product is growing scarcer. Chili powder is made from the ground pods of the chili pepper combined with orégano and other spices. Chili grows in Mexico, but most of it that we use comes from Southern California and the supply is virtually unlimited. One of the important ingredients of Creole cookery, gumbo filé, is a distinctly American spice. The Spanish settlers in Louisiana, unable to find okra (or *gumbo*), discovered that the Indians were using sassafras and so they adopted it, calling it gumbo filé because they had no name for sassafras.

We have learned to appreciate our own cheeses, we are beginning to learn to appreciate our own wines (as far as this country will ever appreciate wine), and now we will learn to use and like our own spices.

❀ ❀

SPICE COOKERY

❊❊❊❊❊❊❊❊❊❊❊❊❊❊❊❊❊❊❊❊❊❊❊❊❊❊❊❊❊❊❊

*Spice, n. & v.t. Aromatic or pungent vege-
table substance used to flavour food, e.g.
cloves, pepper, mace; ss. collectively, as*
dealer in s. sugar & s. & all that's nice, *so spicery (1) n.; (fig.) smack, dash, flavour, (of
malice &c. in person's character, writings,
&c.);* spicebush, *aromatic American shrub
of laurel family; (v.t.) flavour with s.*
[*(vb f.n.) f. O F espice spice f. L Species*]

Concise Oxford Dictionary

COLD TOMATO SOUP

To a No. 3 can of tomatoes add two stalks of celery, one
onion and one bay leaf. When this has boiled for half an hour,
press through a fine sieve and return to the fire. Bring to a
boil and thicken with two tablespoons of sago. Stir until the
sago is thoroughly dissolved and then add a quarter teaspoon
of dry ginger and an eighth teaspoon of allspice. The soup
must be served very cold. Put a teaspoon of sour cream, a slice
of hard boiled egg, a slice of radish, and a slice of cucumber
into each plate before serving.

Rhea Wells made this soup for me one day while drawing
the illustrations for his ever popular "Pepi the Duck," and
good it is too.

❊❊❊❊❊❊❊❊❊❊❊❊❊❊❊❊❊❊❊❊❊❊❊❊❊❊❊❊❊❊

❊❊❊❊❊❊❊❊❊❊❊❊❊❊❊❊❊❊❊❊❊❊❊❊❊❊❊❊

*Make haste, my beloved, and be thou like to
a roe or to a young hart upon the mountain
of spices.*

Song of Solomon 8:14

BISHOP

I wonder how many there are who still know how to make
ginger and root beer. And what happened to the "cups" that
were so popular at the turn of the century? And who remem-
bers "Tiger's Milk" that was made with milk, peach brandy,
and apple-jack? Bishop was of the same vintage.

Wipe and polish a large lemon and a large, firm orange, and
stick them all over with cloves and bits of stick cinnamon in
the rinds. Set them in a pan with a little water, sugar, powdered cinnamon, cloves, allspice, and mace. Roast them for two
hours in a slow oven. Then boil a bottle of Zinfandel (the
recipe, you see, hails from California), sweeten slightly and
add the juice of half a lemon. Put the roasted fruit together
with the spices into the wine. Grate a little nutmeg over the
top and serve as hot as you can.

❊❊❊❊❊❊❊❊❊❊❊❊❊❊❊❊❊❊❊❊❊❊❊❊❊❊❊

✻✻✻✻✻✻✻✻✻✻✻✻✻✻✻✻✻✻✻✻✻✻✻✻✻✻✻✻✻

No one could make pot-pourri like my grandmother. She knew the fragrance value of such combinations as sweet briar, bay, myrtle, lavender and thyme. And she knew to the last fraction of an ounce how much cinnamon, cloves, lemon rind, nutmeg and orris root should be added to the bay salt and saltpetre in which the leaves were "pickled."

Maura Laverty: Never No More

LINZERTORTE

Cream one cup of butter with one cup of sugar until light. Add the beaten yolks of two eggs, a half pound of grated, unblanched almonds, and the grated rind of one lemon. Sift two cups of flour with one tablespoon of cinnamon and half a teaspoon of cloves. Combine both mixtures and roll out to one-half inch thickness. Place into a cake pan (a spring-form is good if you have one) and spread with raspberry jam. Lay strips of dough lattice fashion over the top and bake in a moderate oven for thirty to forty minutes. Raspberry jam is traditional and no other kind should be used. One of the virtues of this cake is that it will keep for at least a week.

✻✻✻✻✻✻✻✻✻✻✻✻✻✻✻✻✻✻✻✻✻✻✻✻✻✻✻✻✻

✳ ✳

Spaniards, exploring from Quito, had found in forests on the eastern slopes of the Andes trees with spicy nuts and fragrant leaves which they thought were cinnamon trees.

Peck: Pageant of South American History

MUSTARD SAUCE

There are sauces galore, and the number of mustard sauces must be legion. This cold sauce is particularly good with hot, boiled fish. Mix the yolks of three hard boiled eggs with the raw yolk of one. Add two tablespoons of prepared mustard, a pinch of salt, and a little scraped onion, three tablespoons of vinegar, seven tablespoons of oil and, finally, two tablespoons of heavy cream. This sauce requires a good deal of stirring so that it may be perfectly smooth.

✳ ✳

SPICE COOKERY

❋❋❋❋❋❋❋❋❋❋❋❋❋❋❋❋❋❋❋❋❋❋❋❋❋❋❋❋❋❋

*Make your transparent Sweet-meats truly
 nice
With Indian Sugar and Arabian Spice;
And let your various Creams incircl'd be
With swelling fruit just ravish'd from the
 Tree.*

King: The Art of Cookery

TURKISH RICE

The delicate flavor of this dish is derived from an onion "incircl'd" with whole cloves. Melt two tablespoons of butter in a frying pan; add one cup of rice and brown to a golden color. When rice begins to brown watch and stir constantly. At the last add one whole onion and sauté till soft. Turn into a casserole and stick whole cloves into the onion and thrust it into the center of the rice. Add three cups of stock, cover, and bake till the rice is cooked; thoroughly soft but each grain separate. Add more stock if necessary during the cooking. There should be no un-absorbed stock.

This is one of Mrs. Richards Taylor's excellent recipes and her directions should be followed carefully.

❋❋❋❋❋❋❋❋❋❋❋❋❋❋❋❋❋❋❋❋❋❋❋❋❋❋❋❋❋❋

✳ ✳

Allspice is the only major spice produced exclusively in the Western Hemisphere. Practically all of it comes from the Island of Jamaica.

GREEN TOMATO CHUTNEY

Mrs. John Wulf, one of the best cooks I know, taught me how to make this. Chop twelve medium-sized green tomatoes and sprinkle them with two tablespoons of salt. Allow them to stand overnight. Dissolve two tablespoons of salt in six cups of vinegar. Chop up eighteen tart apples, two hot red peppers (after removing the seeds), half a pound of green ginger, and three Spanish onions. Drain the tomatoes and mix with the other ingredients, add three cups of seedless raisins, one bunch of celery, and one and a half pounds of brown sugar, and one quarter cup of mustard seed. Cook slowly until the vegetables are tender—this will take about half an hour. Pour into hot jars and seal.

✳ ✳

❋❋❋❋❋❋❋❋❋❋❋❋❋❋❋❋❋❋❋❋❋❋❋❋❋❋❋❋❋

The iuyce of the Mustard seede taken divers mornings fasting doth procure a good memorie. The water of the hearbe and seedes distilled in a Tinne Limbecke heateth the marrow in the bones, if they be often rubbed with the same.

Anonymous

CURRIED EGGS

One of the first cookery books I bought years ago was Henrietta Sowle's "I Go A-Marketing" and it is still one of my favorites. Now long out of print, it does turn up at the nice booksellers from time to time, and you would do well to snap one up. This is "Henriette's" recipe for a simple egg dish and it can be prepared in any pan should you lack the chafing-dish indicated.

Melt in the chafing-dish two ounces of butter, and fry in it two small onions, sliced; take these out and stir in a dessert-spoonful of curry powder and a teaspoonful of Worcestershire sauce. When these are well mixed add half a dozen well-beaten eggs. Cook quickly and serve.

❋❋❋❋❋❋❋❋❋❋❋❋❋❋❋❋❋❋❋❋❋❋❋❋❋❋❋❋❋

SPICE COOKERY

�֎✾✾✾✾✾✾✾✾✾✾✾✾✾✾✾✾✾✾✾✾✾✾✾✾✾✾✾✾

For palates grown callous almost to disease,
Who peppers the highest is surest to please.

Oliver Goldsmith

GULYÁS

This Hungarian word, which incidentally does *not* mean what most of us think it does, is usually rendered as Goulasch or something close to it. To us it means a stew of some sort with or without paprika. To the Hungarians it means a sort of soup, or better still, a sort of stew of soup-like consistency. I speak with more authority on this particular subject than usual, for I have taken numerous lessons from my friend, Benno de Tèrey, in how to prepare it.

Melt some lard in an iron pot and add two or three red onions sliced. When they have begun to turn yellow, add a dessert-spoon of paprika. Cut your beef into cubes, neither too large nor too small, and place it into the pot. Cover with boiling water and let it cook briskly. Watch carefully and when the water is almost evaporated, cover the meat for the second time with boiling water; repeat this process a third time but reduce your flame so that the meat simmers. At this point add some peeled potatoes also cut into cubes. Salt to taste and serve when the potatoes are done. You may have to add more water if the potatoes absorb too much. There should be plenty of gravy.

✾✾✾✾✾✾✾✾✾✾✾✾✾✾✾✾✾✾✾✾✾✾✾✾✾✾✾✾

SPICE COOKERY

❋❋❋❋❋❋❋❋❋❋❋❋❋❋❋❋❋❋❋❋❋❋❋❋❋❋❋❋

> The armipotent Mars, of lances the al-
> mighty,
> Gave Hector a gift, a gilt nutmeg, a lemon
> —stuck with cloves.
>
> Shakespeare: Love's Labor's Lost

SAUERBRATEN

This is best prepared in the cold winter months when the meat can be allowed to remain in the marinade for at least four days, during which time it should be turned twice a day. Select your piece of meat, eye, round, or your own choice, and place it in a china, pottery, or glass dish. Add one onion quartered, a dozen pepper corns, three bay leaves, three cloves, and a few juniper berries if you have them. Cover the meat with vinegar. On the fourth day, remove the meat, drain, and sear quickly on all sides in hot fat. Add some of the marinade and some water and let the meat simmer until it is tender, anywhere from two and a half to three hours. Taste and authorities differ about adding ginger-snaps, a heel of rye bread, or a piece of genuine honey cake, during the cooking process. Failing all these, you may add a pinch of ginger. When the meat is done, remove as much of the fat from the gravy as possible, thicken if necessary and serve. Noodles or dumplings suit this dish. So does red cabbage.

❋❋❋❋❋❋❋❋❋❋❋❋❋❋❋❋❋❋❋❋❋❋❋❋❋❋❋

✳ ✳

It was a tradition among the Romans that to hang an anise plant near one's pillow prevented bad dreams, and to hold a sprig in the hand warded off an attack of epilepsy.

CINNAMON STARS

Cinnamon stars were my favorite Christmas cakes among the twenty-five varieties which were baked in our house each year. The original recipe required that the dough be stirred for a solid hour and stirred it was. With an electric beater twenty minutes appears to be ample. Our stars were never iced except . . . the occasional pan which was baked too brown or almost black and then, the icing hid our shame.

Take the whites of eight eggs, one pound of sugar, and one pound of grated, unblanched almonds, and two tablespoons of powdered cinnamon. Stir your eggs and sugar for half the required time and then add the grated almonds and the cinnamon. Pat the dough out on a pastry board, strewn with flour *and* sugar, to the thickness of three-eighths of an inch. The dough should be of the consistency that does not permit of rolling. Cut out with a star cutter, bake on buttered tins in a slow oven for about thirty minutes.

✳ ✳

SPICE COOKERY

✻✻✻✻✻✻✻✻✻✻✻✻✻✻✻✻✻✻✻✻✻✻✻✻✻✻✻✻✻✻✻✻

Take almonds unblanched and these you
    bray
Strain them with wine I dare well say;
Thereto add powder of good ginger
And sugar, and boil all these together,
And colour with saffron and salt it wele
And serve it forth Sir at your mele.

Liber Cure Cocorum

GINGER CRISPS

Cream one cup of butter with one cup of sugar until well blended. Add three slightly beaten eggs, one tablespoon of molasses, and one cup of flour. Finally add one teaspoon of cinnamon and half a teaspoon of powdered ginger. Drop by spoonfuls on a buttered baking sheet and spread the heaps thinly. Bake in a moderate oven until crisp.

✻✻✻✻✻✻✻✻✻✻✻✻✻✻✻✻✻✻✻✻✻✻✻✻✻✻✻✻✻✻✻✻

❀ ❀

Take of the best fruits in the lands in your vessels, and carry down the man a present, a little balm, and a little honey, spices and myrrh, nuts and almonds.

Genesis 43:11

CUMBERLAND SAUCE

Cumberland Sauce is the perfect accompaniment for sliced, cold ham. It is not difficult to make and will keep on ice. Mince two shallots as finely as you can. Remove every bit of the white skin of the peel of an orange and cut the peel into minute strips. Place the shallots and the orange rind in a saucepan with a little water and boil for fifteen minutes. Strain off the water. Whip the mixture into six tablespoons of currant (red) jelly. Add a pinch of ginger, a pinch of cayenne, the juice of one lemon and that of one orange. Mix well before serving.

❀ ❀

SPICE COOKERY

✿ ✿

*I must have saffron, to colour the warden-
pies; mace; dates,—nutmegs, seven; a race or
two of ginger,—but that I may beg; four
pounds of prunes, and as many of raisins o'
the sun.*

Shakespeare: The Winter's Tale

PRUNEAUX AU VIN ROUGE

This may sound a bit too extravagant at first, but it is an excellent way to use up rests of red wine. The American wines of the claret or burgundy type are not too expensive to begin with. Soak large prunes in red wine overnight. The next morning boil them in the wine, there should be enough to cover, to which you have added half a cup of sugar, a stick of cinnamon and the thin rind of half a lemon. When the prunes are soft, remove them and let the juice boil a little longer. Serve very cold.

✿ ✿

✳✳✳✳✳✳✳✳✳✳✳✳✳✳✳✳✳✳✳✳✳✳✳✳✳✳✳✳✳✳

For he can thoroughly enjoy
The pepper when he pleases!

Lewis Carroll: Alice in Wonderland

NASTURTIUM SEEDS

There are, I believe, people who say that they can prepare a leg of lamb so that it tastes "just like venison." Why they should want to do this I cannot tell, and I am confident that they fool no one but themselves. Here is Florence White's receipt for pickling nasturtium seeds and I hasten to assure my readers that they taste like very good nasturtium seeds and *not* like capers.

To one quart of white vinegar add one and a half ounces of salt, one shallot, some whole pepper corns, a few pieces of mace, some grated nutmeg and some horseradish. The proper amount of spices can be determined by the individual taste. Boil this for five minutes and then pour it into a glass jar. Cover, and when it is cold, strain off into another glass jar. Keep the jar tightly covered and see to it that the cover is not made of metal and that no metal comes into contact with the spiced vinegar. As the nasturtium blossoms fall gather the seeds and drop them into the pickle. Miss White stresses the fact that seeds should be gathered as soon as the blossoms fall and before they get hard.

✳✳✳✳✳✳✳✳✳✳✳✳✳✳✳✳✳✳✳✳✳✳✳✳✳✳✳✳✳✳

SPICE COOKERY

Like several other very old spices, cinnamon was believed capable of inspiring love, and it was used to concoct love charms.

MULLED WINE

Mulled wines have been favorites for centuries in many lands. It is surprising to note how many recipes direct that the wine be brought to a boil. This is incorrect and it not only affects the flavor of the wine, giving it an unnatural heady quality, but it also affects the drinker on occasion. Another quality of mulled wine is that it does not require a very good or vintage wine. *Au contraire*, it would be a pity to use anything other than an ordinary red wine for this purpose. To each bottle of wine, add a dozen cloves, the thin rind of a lemon, a tablespoon of sugar, and a short length of stick cinnamon. Let all this draw over a low flame for a while, and *not* boil. The wine should be served very hot.

'Tis ever thus with simple folk—an accepted wit has but to say "Pass the mustard," and they roar their ribs out.

William S. Gilbert: Yeomen of the Guard

MIXED SPICES

I can well imagine that there still are people who mix their own spices. Directions for their preparation can be found in more than one modern cookery book. They all seem to be patterned on the recipe given by M. Jules Gouffé in his "Livre de Cuisine" and sometimes they are even called "French Spices," no doubt in deference to the nationality of the originator of the particular formula.

Into a paper bag place one quarter ounce of thyme and a similar quantity of bayleaf, one eighth ounce of marjoram and an equal amount of rosemary. Keep the bag near the back of the stove until the herbs are quite dry. Obviously this refers to fresh herbs, but an almost equal result could be obtained by using the dry variety. Place the dried herbs in a mortar (or mixing bowl) and add one half ounce each of nutmeg and cloves, one quarter ounce of whole pepper, and one eighth ounce of cayenne pepper. Pound the whole, says M. Gouffé, and pass through a hair sieve. Keep in a dry and well-corked bottle.

Mustard is meet for brawne beef or powdered motoun;
verdius to boyled capoun veel chiken or bakon;
And to signet & swan, conveny ant is the chawdon,
Roost beeff & goos with garlek, vinegre, or pepur, in conclusion..

John Russell: The Boke of Nurture

BERMUDA TURTLE SOUP

Put two pounds of turtle to parboil with about three quarts of water. Remove skin, bones, etc., returning the meat and fat to the water. After it has boiled for one and a half hours, add two tablespoons of cassareep (a West Indian condiment made of cassava and spices), half a nutmeg, half a tablespoon of cinnamon, one tablespoon of allspice. Cut up a quarter pound of salt pork, fry it in a pan, adding to it a bouquet of thyme and parsley and half a tablespoon of whole cloves. Put the pork and the herbs in a piece of cheesecloth, tie it up, and put it in the soup. Mix one and a half tablespoons of butter with two tablespoons of flour to a smooth paste, add one and a half tablespoons of Worcestershire sauce gradually, and stir into the soup very slowly. Just before serving, add the juice of half a lemon or a lime, a quarter of a pint of sherry, and a quarter of a cup of brandy.

❋❋❋❋❋❋❋❋❋❋❋❋❋❋❋❋❋❋❋❋❋❋❋❋❋❋❋❋❋

*I have a gammon of bacon and two razes of
ginger, to be deliver'd as far as Charing-
cross.*

Shakespeare: King Henry the Fourth, I

SCRIPTURE CAKE

In the days of our grandmothers, more than one cookery
book contained the recipe for Scripture Cake. It is apparently
unknown to the present generation.

(1) Four and one half cups of 1st Kings iv. 22; (2) one
and one half cups of Judges v. 25; (3) two cups of Jeremiah
vi. 20; (4) two cups of 1st Samuel xxx. 12; (5) two cups of
Nahum iii. 12; (6) one cup of Numbers xvii. 8; (7) two
tablespoons of 1st Samuel xiv. 25; (8) six articles of Jeremiah
xvii. 11; (9) a pinch of Leviticus ii. 12; (10) a teaspoon of
Amos iv. 5; (11) season to taste with 2nd Chronicles ix. 9;
add citron and follow Solomon's advice for making a good
boy; (12) Proverbs xxiii. 14 and you will have a good cake.

❋❋❋❋❋❋❋❋❋❋❋❋❋❋❋❋❋❋❋❋❋❋❋❋❋❋❋❋❋

SPICE COOKERY

✸✸✸✸✸✸✸✸✸✸✸✸✸✸✸✸✸✸✸✸✸✸✸✸✸✸

And spice, and oil for the light, and for the anointing oil, and for the sweet incense.

Exodus 36:28

PRUNE ICE CREAM

Soften one teaspoon of granulated gelatin in one tablespoon of cold water. Scald a large can of evaporated milk and dissolve the gelatin in it. Add one quarter teaspoon of cinnamon, one eighth teaspoon of powdered nutmeg, one eighth teaspoon of cloves, and a pinch of salt. Mix well and chill. Remove the pits from two cups of cooked prunes and cut them into pieces. Whip the chilled milk until thick, add the prunes and three tablespoons of brown sugar. Pour into a tray of the refrigerating unit and freeze until set, which may take from three to four hours.

✸✸✸✸✸✸✸✸✸✸✸✸✸✸✸✸✸✸✸✸✸✸✸✸✸

❋ ❋

Chewing a clove to sweeten the breath is a custom which was begun by the ancient Chinese.

GINGER CUPCAKES

Stir one half cup of sugar into two-thirds of a cup of molasses and add one half cup of butter, one teaspoon of ginger and one teaspoon of cinnamon. Bring this to the boiling point, remove from fire and cool. Sift together two cups of flour and one teaspoon of baking powder. Beat two eggs and add them to the molasses mixture, alternating with the flour and one cup of sour milk. Beat well after each addition. Bake in greased muffin pan in a moderate oven for about fifteen minutes.

❋ ❋

SPICE COOKERY

❋❋❋❋❋❋❋❋❋❋❋❋❋❋❋❋❋❋❋❋❋❋❋❋❋❋❋❋

Wytteth wel that the Notmuge berethe the Maces. In time of ripenesse the huske of the fruit cleaveth of its selfe and showeth his Mace, which then is of a perfect crimson colour and make a most goodly stew. It is good against freckles in the face and quickeneth the sight.

John Mandeville

MARROW BALLS

These are a delicate accompaniment for clear soups and, with a little practice, they are not difficult to make. The main point is not to use too many bread crumbs or the balls will be tough.

Remove the marrow from two bones which should give you about half a cup. It will be an easier task if you ask the butcher to saw the bones into two or three sections. Work it with a fork until it becomes smooth, add one beaten egg, a dash of salt, a teaspoon of parsley chopped as fine as you can, and finally a generous sprinkling of freshly grated nutmeg. Add enough bread crumbs so that the mixture will hold together. It is a good plan to try one out to see if it will hold its shape. Boil in the soup and they will rise to the surface when done.

❋❋❋❋❋❋❋❋❋❋❋❋❋❋❋❋❋❋❋❋❋❋❋❋❋❋❋❋

SPICE COOKERY

✿ ✿

He who has plenty of pepper will pepper his cabbage.

Publius Syrus: Maxims

PHILADELPHIA PEPPER POT

Cover four pounds of tripe with four quarts of cold water in a large soup pot. Add two leeks, three carrots, two sprigs of parsley, a sprig of thyme, two large onions, one teaspoon of allspice, one teaspoon of whole cloves, one tablespoon of marjoram, one tablespoon of summer savory, and one red pepper. Bring this to a boil and let it simmer for about four hours. In another pot, place a well washed veal knuckle covered with six cups of water. Bring this to a boil and let it simmer until the other broth is done. Remove the knuckle and add the veal broth to the other. Remove the tripe and cut it into small pieces. Return to the pot, add one potato cubed, and cook until soft. Make a roux of two tablespoons of butter and three tablespoons of flour as well as some of the broth. When it is smooth add it to the soup. Pepper Pot is usually served with little meat or flour dumplings.

✿ ✿

✻✻✻✻✻✻✻✻✻✻✻✻✻✻✻✻✻✻✻✻✻✻✻✻✻✻✻✻✻

The whole race of Yankee peddlers in particular are proverbial for dishonesty.... They warrant broken watches to be the best time-keepers in the world; sell pinchbeck trinkets for gold; and always have a large assortment of wooden nutmegs and stagnant barometers.

Thomas Hamilton: Men and Manners in America

COMPANY MEAT LOAF

Mix two pounds of ground beef, one pound of ground pork, one small can of tomato paste, one beaten egg, and half a cup of sour cream, and season with salt, pepper, and freshly ground nutmeg. "Now," said Thyra Samter Winslow, for this is her recipe, "draw a line."

Soak half a loaf of bread in water for a few minutes and drain it thoroughly. Add a teaspoon of grated onion, half a cup of sour cream, one beaten egg, salt, pepper, and half a teaspoon of poultry seasoning. Place half your meat mixture in a greased loaf pan, then your bread stuffing, and the other half of the meat on top. Cover with bread crumbs and some chopped bacon. Bake in a moderate oven for fifty minutes. Decorate with slices of hard boiled egg.

✻✻✻✻✻✻✻✻✻✻✻✻✻✻✻✻✻✻✻✻✻✻✻✻✻✻✻✻

✽ ✽

The natives of the Spice Islands prized the clove trees not always for their spice value but as a record of ages, it being a custom to plant a clove tree for each child that was born.

CURRY SALAD DRESSING

A pleasant variant of the usual French dressing is one made with curry. Using your favorite dressing recipe add half as much curry powder as you do salt, or use the following proportions: two tablespoons of vinegar to four of oil, half a teaspoon of salt, a quarter of a teaspoon of curry powder, a little grated onion or one quarter of a teaspoon of onion juice. See that your curry powder is well dissolved.

✽ ✽

❀ ❀

Ginger, the root of a herbaceous perennial flourishing in tropical and semi-tropical countries, is one of the few spices which grow below ground.

GAZPACHO

This is an excellent Spanish dish for a hot summer evening. In most American cookery books, when it is found, it is usually misspelled as Gaspacho. Sheila Hibben cites a variant popular in Florida known as Guspachy. In any case, Gazpacho, pronounced gath-pah'-tcho, is made as follows. After you have removed the crusts, put four slices of white bread, cut into cubes, into a soup tureen. Mince one clove of garlic, slice one onion, slice one cucumber, shred two green peppers, and add all of this to the bread in the tureen. Season with salt, coarsely ground black pepper, a little dry mustard, and some caraway seeds. Pour olive oil over the bread and vegetables and mix thoroughly. Then pour over six cups of water to which you have added two tablespoons of vinegar and the juice of half a lemon. Put on the ice for three or four hours. It is served in the tureen with small pieces of ice swimming in it.

❀ ❀

✻ ✻

Nutmegs are gathered by means of a long pole to which is attached a basket and prongs. The basket arrangement in the East is called gai gai and is manipulated with amazing dexterity by the natives.

BAKED INDIAN PUDDING

Scald one pint of milk and sprinkle into it one half cup of yellow corn meal. Cook this for about ten minutes, stirring carefully; add one cup of molasses and cook for another five minutes. Remove from the stove and stir in one teaspoon of butter, a teaspoon of sugar, half a teaspoon of cinnamon, and half a teaspoon of ginger. Bake in a buttered dish for two hours in a slow oven.

It is traditional to serve hard sauce with Indian Pudding but at the Hartwell Farm, between Lexington and Concord, it is dished up with a generous helping of vanilla ice-cream.

✻ ✻

❋❋❋❋❋❋❋❋❋❋❋❋❋❋❋❋❋❋❋❋❋❋❋❋❋❋❋❋

When Magellan started out to encircle the world, the voyage took years and was completed by an assistant. All but one of the ships foundered, but that one had enough pepper on board to pay for all the lost boats and yield a profit besides.

FRUIT COOKIES

Cream together one half cup of butter, one half cup of white sugar and one half cup of brown. Add one egg and beat well. Then add one tablespoon of molasses, one half teaspoon of cloves and one half teaspoon of nutmeg. Stir one third of a teaspoon of soda into one third of a cup of sour cream. Add this to the mixture alternately with two cups of flour. Finally add a half cup of chopped nuts and a half cup of chopped raisins. Drop teaspoonfuls on a cookie sheet, well apart, and bake in a hot oven for about ten minutes.

❋❋❋❋❋❋❋❋❋❋❋❋❋❋❋❋❋❋❋❋❋❋❋❋❋❋❋❋

❋ ❋

(1794) Oct. 20, Monday. Busy most part of the Afternoon in making some Mead Wine, to fourteen Pound of Honey, I put four Gallons of Water, boiled it more than an hour with Ginger and two handfulls of dried Elder-Flowers in it, and skimmed it well.

James Woodforde: Diary of a Country Parson

BROWN BETTY

Cube two cups of bread with the crusts removed, and pare and chop enough apples to make three cups. Melt three tablespoons of butter in a skillet and add the bread cubes stirring well until they are all covered with the butter. Mix a quarter of a teaspoon of cinnamon with a quarter of a teaspoon of nutmeg and half a cup of sugar. Put one quarter of the buttered crumbs in a baking dish, and over them half of the apples. Sprinkle this with half the spiced sugar. Add another quarter of crumbs, the rest of the apples. Sprinkle the grated rind of one lemon and then pour over the juice together with a quarter of a cup of water. Cover with the remaining crumbs and grate a little nutmeg over the top. Bake, covered, in a medium oven for three quarters of an hour. Uncover and brown it quickly. Serve with plain, heavy cream.

❋ ❋

* *

I sing of dews, of rains, and piece by piece
Of balm, of oil, or spice, of ambergris

Robert Herrick

POPPY SEED CRESCENTS

It is interesting to read in an early work on cookery that, "however beautiful the flowers of the poppy plant (*papaver somniferum*) may be, and however serviceable for table decoration, they are not suitable for culinary purposes, because of their somniferous influence, due to the opium contained in the juice." Be that as it may, here we use the seeds and not the flowers for those delicacies known in Austria as *Mohn-Kipferl.*

Boil one half a cup of ground poppy seeds, one half a cup of sugar, one tablespoon of butter, one half a teaspoon of cinnamon, and the grated rind of half a lemon, with enough milk to make a fairly stiff paste. Roll out a yeast dough to the thickness of half an inch, and cut out triangles. Fill each triangle with some of the poppy seed paste (which should have been cooled in the meantime) and roll the large end towards the small. Place on a baking sheet and curve the ends to form a crescent. Brush with the yolk of an egg beaten with a little water. Let them rise until double their size, and bake in a hot oven for twenty minutes.

✻✻✻✻✻✻✻✻✻✻✻✻✻✻✻✻✻✻✻✻✻✻✻✻✻✻✻

Saffron is the stigma of the crocus sativa.
*Each crocus-like flower yields but three
saffron stigma and it takes about 225,000 of
these to make a pound of saffron.*

ANIS PLÄTZCHEN

This is another famous Christmas cake, *Plätzchen* meaning
a lozenge, and when they are baked they puff up and look like
so many mushrooms with their stems cut off.

Stir three eggs with one cup of sugar for half an hour. This
is the time given in the original recipe and if you use an electric beater, ten minutes will suffice. Add one cup of pastry
flour and three teaspoons of aniseed. Drop on a buttered baking sheet and let them stand over night. Bake in a moderate
oven for about ten minutes.

✻✻✻✻✻✻✻✻✻✻✻✻✻✻✻✻✻✻✻✻✻✻✻✻✻✻✻

SPICE COOKERY

✽✽✽✽✽✽✽✽✽✽✽✽✽✽✽✽✽✽✽✽✽✽✽✽✽✽✽✽✽✽

Take thou also unto thee principal spices, of pure myrrh five hundred shekels, and of sweet cinnamon half so much, even two hundred and fifty shekels, and of sweet calamus two hundred and fifty shekels.

Exodus 30:23

APPLE SAUCE CAKE

Cream half a cup of butter with one cup of sugar and then add one cup of cold apple sauce. Then mix together one cup of flour, one half teaspoon of soda, one teaspoon of cloves, one teaspoon of cinnamon. Add this to the rest and finally, half a cup of raisins cut fine and half a cup of chopped nuts. Bake in a buttered loaf pan in a moderate oven for fifty minutes.

✽✽✽✽✽✽✽✽✽✽✽✽✽✽✽✽✽✽✽✽✽✽✽✽✽✽✽✽✽✽

✾✾✾✾✾✾✾✾✾✾✾✾✾✾✾✾✾✾✾✾✾✾✾✾✾✾✾✾

Allspice grows on trees twenty to thirty feet tall, and its name is due to its flavor which resembles a combination of cloves, cinnamon, and nutmeg.

CAFÉ BRÛLOT

Take one cup of cognac, thirty lumps of sugar, forty whole cloves, the thin peel of half a lemon and half an orange. Place this in a brûlot bowl, if you have one, and in a china bowl if you do not. Place a little of the mixture in a silver ladle, add one lump of sugar, and set it afire. This is accomplished more easily if a match is held under the bowl of the ladle for several seconds. Slowly lower the flaming ladle into the bowl until the contents catches fire. When it has burned a few moments, add your coffee slowly. A brûlot bowl has a spirit lamp under it which simplifies matters somewhat.

✾✾✾✾✾✾✾✾✾✾✾✾✾✾✾✾✾✾✾✾✾✾✾✾✾✾✾✾

❄❄❄❄❄❄❄❄❄❄❄❄❄❄❄❄❄❄❄❄❄❄❄❄❄❄❄❄

In English pubs and inns, ginger was found on the shelf so that it might be sprinkled into the ale and porter, stirred with a red hot poker and drunk sizzling hot.

PICKLED EGGS

Remove the shells from sixteen hard boiled eggs and place them in mason jars. Boil one quart of vinegar (a red wine vinegar is perfect) for ten minutes together with half an ounce of black pepper corns, half an ounce of allspice, half an ounce of ginger and half an ounce of cloves. Pour the boiling vinegar over the eggs and when they are cold, cover tightly and store in a cool dry place. They will be ready for use in about two weeks and are delicious with cold meats.

❄❄❄❄❄❄❄❄❄❄❄❄❄❄❄❄❄❄❄❄❄❄❄❄❄❄❄❄

❋ ❋

Ground mace is a yellow powder with a fragrance like nutmeg. It comes honestly by this aroma, for mace is the fleshy aril which grows around the nutmeg.

SPICED CHERRIES

These are simple to make providing you like to pit cherries. The large black cherries are the best. When they have been pitted, take one pound of sugar for each pound of fruit. For each five pounds of fruit, take one teaspoon of cinnamon, one teaspoon of allspice, half a teaspoon of ground cloves, and a few whole cloves. Boil until thick and seal at once in mason jars.

❋ ❋

SPICE COOKERY

❀ ❀

Pepper vines are trained to climb poles like a grape vine. From two to three years after planting the berries appear, full bearing being attained at the age of seven or eight years.

CHICKEN CURRY SOUP

This is a soup to be made whenever you have occasion to use boiled chicken. But do not make the mistake of serving chicken *and* chicken soup at the same meal. Boil your chicken in your accustomed manner, adding one onion and several stalks of celery to the water. You must have just enough water to cover the chicken so that your stock may have sufficient strength. Set it aside to cool (overnight is best) and then carefully remove every trace of fat. To each quart of stock add one teaspoon of curry powder and one pint of rich milk, or better still, heavy cream. See that your curry powder is well dissolved in some of the stock. Serve very cold with a few minced chives in each plate.

❀ ❀

� � � � � � � � � � � � � � � � � � � � � � � � � �

*Dost thou think because thou art virtuous,
there shall be no more cakes and ale?
Yes, by Saint Anne; and ginger shall be
hot i' the mouth too.*

Shakespeare: Twelfth Night

BOILED SPICED TONGUE

Boil the tongue until nearly tender. Cut off the root, skin, and rub it over with a mixture of one teaspoon of allspice, half a teaspoon of ginger and half a teaspoon of black pepper. Dredge with flour. Fry a sliced onion in two tablespoons of butter and then brown the tongue in the butter. Place the tongue into a saucepan. In the butter in the pan, brown a tablespoon of flour and add two cups of water and stir till smooth. Pour this over the tongue, add half a cup of raisins and one cup of vinegar. Simmer until the tongue is tender.

✻ ✻

SPICE COOKERY

❀ ❀

In Zanzibar the natives believe that when the clove tree which was planted at a man's birth dies, the man will soon die too.

CURRIED CARROTS

It is said that eating carrots improves one's visibility at night. True or false, here is an interesting manner of preparing them.

Boil young carrots until tender and then cut them in quarters lengthwise. They should have been cooked in no more than a cup of water. Make a roux of one tablespoon of butter and one tablespoon of flour and one cup of heavy cream. Add the carrot water to this and season with a pinch of salt, a pinch of black pepper and one teaspoon of curry powder. Pour over carrots and serve.

❀ ❀

❀❀❀❀❀❀❀❀❀❀❀❀❀❀❀❀❀❀❀❀❀❀❀❀❀❀❀❀❀❀

Nutmegs are tested by bouncing them and the resulting sound shows if they are good and solid, or damaged and wormy.

BARBECUE SAUCE

Mince an onion and fry it in three tablespoons of butter. Add two cloves of garlic, one tablespoon of sugar, one teaspoon of salt, one teaspoon of chili powder, one teaspoon of black pepper, one tablespoon of paprika, half a tablespoon of dry mustard. When this is well mixed, add two cups of meat stock, one cup of vinegar, a dash of tabasco and one teaspoon of Worcestershire sauce. Simmer for an hour and, when strained, use it to baste your meat.

❀❀❀❀❀❀❀❀❀❀❀❀❀❀❀❀❀❀❀❀❀❀❀❀❀❀❀❀❀❀

SPICE COOKERY

❀❀❀❀❀❀❀❀❀❀❀❀❀❀❀❀❀❀❀❀❀❀❀❀❀❀❀❀

*At one time the Dutch destroyed all the nut-
meg trees and seedlings in all of their pos-
sessions except the island of Amboyna, so
that they could control the production of
the precious spice.*

PORCUPINES

Select hard, firm, ripe pears and peel them carefully, leav-
ing the stem on. Boil them slowly in a heavy sugar syrup to
which you have added a few whole cloves, a pinch of ginger,
and several lengths of stick cinnamon. When the pears are
tender (they must be whole) remove them carefully. Blanch
a handful of almonds and split and then cut them into thin
slivers. Starting at the top of each pear, stick the almond
slivers in at intervals of an eighth of an inch until the whole
pear is properly studded. This takes both time and patience
but the result is well worth the trouble. A little red wine may
be added to your syrup while the pears are cooking which will
give them a pleasing color.

❀❀❀❀❀❀❀❀❀❀❀❀❀❀❀❀❀❀❀❀❀❀❀❀❀❀❀❀

❋❋❋❋❋❋❋❋❋❋❋❋❋❋❋❋❋❋❋❋❋❋❋❋❋❋❋❋

There are records of cinnamon having been used in China two thousand years before the birth of Christ.

CHILI SAUCE

Peel and slice twelve tomatoes and place them in a preserving kettle together with two large onions and two red peppers which you have chopped up. Cook slowly for about three hours, stirring from time to time. During the last hour of cooking add three tablespoons of sugar, one tablespoon of salt, two teaspoons of cloves, two teaspoons of cinnamon, two teaspoons of grated nutmeg and a dash of cayenne.

❋❋❋❋❋❋❋❋❋❋❋❋❋❋❋❋❋❋❋❋❋❋❋❋❋❋❋❋

SPICE COOKERY

❊ ❊

After meat comes mustard; or, like money
to a starving man at sea, when there are no
victuals to be bought with it.

Cervantes: Don Quixote

SAFFRON RICE

Saffron, an expensive spice, usually comes in little envelopes and each one holds about a "pinch." The local Italian grocer is where you have the best chance of buying it. Saffron should never be added to anything in its dry state, but always dissolved in some of the liquid in which you intend using it.

Cook one cup of rice in two cups of good stock. To wash or not to wash the rice—is a matter for your own conscience and culinary training. The grains should be done but not mushy. Add two pinches of saffron, previously dissolved, and a half cup of melted butter. Toss well but do not break the rice and serve at once.

❊ ❊

✳ ✳

No book is serviceable until it has been read, and re-read, and loved, and loved again; and marked, so that you can refer to the passages you want in it, as a soldier can seize the weapon he needs in an armory, or a housewife bring the spice she needs from her store.

John Ruskin

CHEESE SPREAD

Take half a pound of cottage cheese, or three Philadelphia cream cheeses, and mix it well with an electric beater. Add one tablespoon of soft butter, a generous dash of salt, an equally generous dash of paprika and half a cup of heavy, sour cream. Mix for at least ten minutes and then add a teaspoon of caraway seeds.

Spread on thin slices of genuine, black pumpernickel and served with black radishes this is a veritable treat. Black radishes are hard to come by and you may be surprised that your local Chinese laundryman may be able to tell you where to find them. Properly served, they are peeled and sliced very thin, down to the root but not cut through. Spread salt between each slice and skewer them tightly with two toothpicks and permit them to draw for at least an hour.

✳ ✳

It is believed that turmeric, an essential ingredient of curry powder, is rich in vitamins as are other vegetables of high colors like carrots and paprika.

SCRAMBLED EGGS À L'INDIENNE

Peel, core and cut into little slivers two apples. Mince two onions and fry them, together with the apple slivers, in three tablespoons of butter. When the apples are almost cooked stir in half a tablespoon of curry powder, a little salt and a little pepper. When this is ready prepare your scrambled eggs. Keep them soft, add the curry and a tablespoon of chutney. Serve on toast.

✳ ✳

Ground pepper spread on rugs to be stored or in woolens, is a moth-repellant known around the world.

LA BOUILLABAISSE

Garlic? . . . well, a little, merely to be traditional. But very little I tell you, a whisp, a souvenir, hardly remembered.

Saffron? Not bad, but again, not too much. However, enough to gild your fingers when you put it in.

Fish? . . . Of course, but fish of fine flavor, caught then and there, and lobster and whiting, and above all, rascasse.

Oil? One must have that as well. But of the very best, bearing the aroma to the nostril.

Thyme, rosemary, fennel, and parsley put in, tied in a little sack, gently, appetizingly.

Let the whole cook; cut up fresh bread into thick slices; and perhaps, just perhaps, you may have bouillabaisse.

But that it may be real, good and without fault, a miracle must be, for more than fish, saffron, fennel, it needs the air of Marseille!

Freely translated from the French of Jacques Normand.

✳ ✳

SPICE COOKERY

✳ ✳

Throughout Central and South America all-spice is known as Jamaica pepper because the appearance suggests certain varieties of whole black pepper. In the spice trade it is called pimento, not to be confused with pimiento.

SZÉKELYGULYÁS

Cut two pounds of pork, half lean and half fat, into inch cubes. Heat two tablespoons of fat and brown in it two sliced onions. Add one teaspoon of paprika and then the meat and let the meat brown without sticking to the pan. Add water in small quantities from time to time until the meat is tender, the whole process requiring about one hour. Boil two pounds of sauerkraut in another pot and when it is tender add it to the meat, being careful to first drain off all of the water. At this point add your salt, one cup of sour cream and a tablespoon of caraway seeds. Let it boil for a few minutes and serve.

✳ ✳

❋ ❋

The seeds and bulbs of saffron were so jealously guarded in its native country that to part with either was to incur danger of being put to death.

Florence White: Flowers as Food

ALMOND SOUP

This is a Spanish dish and its native name is *Sopa de Almendras*. Grind half a pound of blanched almonds, reserving a few to be sliced into thin slivers. Take one quart of stock, preferably half chicken and half veal, and add a pinch of mace, three cloves, a little grated nutmeg, a teaspoon of paprika, a sprig of thyme, and a pinch of dry mustard. Allow this to simmer for half an hour and then add your ground almonds stirring well until they are thoroughly blended in the soup. Just before removing from the fire add one cup of scalded cream but do not let the soup boil once this has been added. Add the almond slivers and serve.

❋ ❋

Anise was a favourite ingredient in the Roman cuisine. The Roman epicures ate aniseed cakes to promote digestion and it was much praised by Pliny.

Edith Wheelwright: The Physick Garden

MOUSAKA

Mousaka is the Bulgarian word for eggplant and they prepare it in a number of interesting and delectable fashions, one of which follows.

Slice an eggplant into thicknesses of one and a half inch without removing the skin, salt each piece and let it draw for an hour. Drain off the salt and wash the pieces. Chop three medium onions and fry them in three tablespoons of lard, add salt and black pepper, half a teaspoon of paprika and a teaspoon of nutmeg and two chopped tomatoes. Then add one pound of beef chopped and half a pound of pork, also chopped. When this has cooked for a few minutes, place some of it in a baking pan, cover with a few slices of the eggplant, more meat, more eggplant and finally a layer of the meat. Add a little water, and bake in a medium oven for one hour.

✻ ✻

Pepper was known to the Greeks, and was one of the chief spices in the trade of the Middle Ages, when tribute was levied in "pepper rents."

SPICE CAKE

Mix and sift together two cups of flour, one teaspoon of baking powder, half a teaspoon of soda, one teaspoon of cloves, one teaspoon of nutmeg, and half a teaspoon of mace. Cream half a cup of sweet butter and when smooth, add one cup of sugar, continue stirring and then add three eggs well beaten. Mix one cup of molasses with a quarter cup of milk and add this alternately with the mixed flour. Bake in a buttered pan in a moderate oven for about fifty minutes.

✻ ✻

SPICE COOKERY

❋❋❋❋❋❋❋❋❋❋❋❋❋❋❋❋❋❋❋❋❋❋❋❋❋❋❋❋❋❋❋❋

Peter Piper picked a peck of pickled pepper;
A peck of pickled pepper Peter Piper
picked;
If Peter Piper picked a peck of pickled
pepper,
Where's the peck of pickled pepper that
Peter Piper picked?

Old Nursery Rhyme

PFEFFERNÜSSE

Beat together four eggs and two cups of sugar for one hour (a quarter of the time if using an electric beater). Then add one quarter pound of finely shredded citron, two teaspoons of cinnamon, one teaspoon of allspice, one teaspoon of cloves, one teaspoon of aniseed, one tablespoon of crushed cardamom seeds and half a teaspoon of black pepper. When this is mixed add four cups of sifted pastry flour. Let the dough rest for an hour and then shape into small balls the size of a walnut. Let them stand overnight, and then brush them with a mixture of one cup of confectioner's sugar and one quarter cup of milk. Place on baking sheet and bake in a moderate oven for about twenty minutes.

❋❋❋❋❋❋❋❋❋❋❋❋❋❋❋❋❋❋❋❋❋❋❋❋❋❋❋❋❋❋❋

❋❋❋❋❋❋❋❋❋❋❋❋❋❋❋❋❋❋❋❋❋❋❋❋❋❋❋❋❋❋

The Mustard seedes retained under the tongue prevaile against the palsey of the tongue.

Anonymous

WASSAIL BOWL

This is an old English drink served at Christmas time. Put half a pound of loaf sugar in a large bowl, grate a nutmeg over it, and dust over one teaspoon of powdered ginger and one of cinnamon; pour over this one pint of hot beer, half a pint of sherry and five pints of cold beer. Stir this thoroughly and let it stand for two or three hours. Cut three thin slices of bread and toast them brown, cut them into pieces, and put them in the bowl. Core and roast six apples until they are well done and add them to the bowl.

❋❋❋❋❋❋❋❋❋❋❋❋❋❋❋❋❋❋❋❋❋❋❋❋❋❋❋❋❋❋

✿✿✿✿✿✿✿✿✿✿✿✿✿✿✿✿✿✿✿✿✿✿✿✿✿✿✿✿✿✿✿

When you are layd in bed so softe
A cage of gold shal hange alofte,
Wythe longe peper fayre burning
And cloves that be swete smellyng,
Frankinsense and olibanum,
That when ye slepe, the taste may come,
And yf ye no rest can take
All nyght mynstrels for you shall wake.

The Squire of Low Degree

LAMB CHOPS MARINADE

Soak kidney lamb chops in the following mixture for twelve hours: Four tablespoons olive oil, one tablespoon tarragon vinegar, one small sliced onion, one mashed clove of garlic, one bay leaf, twelve whole black pepper corns, six cloves, one saltspoon of salt, two teaspoons of dried thyme, a few sprigs of parsley, and the rind of one lemon. Drain the chops and broil them to the degree you like.

✿✿✿✿✿✿✿✿✿✿✿✿✿✿✿✿✿✿✿✿✿✿✿✿✿✿✿✿✿✿✿

❀ ❀

Off at sea north-east winds blow
Sabaean odours from the spicy shore
Of Araby the blest.

Milton: Paradise Lost

ANISEED CAKES

Sift together four cups of flour, one cup of sugar and half a teaspoon of salt. Add three quarters of a cup of aniseed and work in two cups of butter as you would in making pie dough. Add two eggs and when your dough is mixed, roll it out and cut into various shapes and bake in moderate oven for about twenty minutes.

❀ ❀

SPICE COOKERY

❀❀❀❀❀❀❀❀❀❀❀❀❀❀❀❀❀❀❀❀❀❀❀❀❀❀❀❀❀❀

*With the iuyce of Licorice, Ginger, and
other spices, there is made certaine bread or
cakes called Ginger-bread, which is cast into
mouldes, some of one fashion, and some of
another.*

Anonymous

HIPPOCRAS

This is said to have been named after Hippocrates because
of his fondness for it. It was formerly much used in England.
The original Hippocras is described as a mixture of Lisbon
and Canary wines sweetened with sugar and flavored with
spices and aromatics.

Mix one gallon of sauterne with half a gallon of chablis.
Mix three ounces of stick cinnamon, three ounces of ginger,
half an ounce of grated nutmeg, half an ounce of cloves, half
an ounce of coriander seed, and two pounds of sugar. Let this
stand over night and then add two more pounds of sugar and
one pint of milk. Mix well and strain through a fine cloth.
Bottle and cork.

❀❀❀❀❀❀❀❀❀❀❀❀❀❀❀❀❀❀❀❀❀❀❀❀❀❀❀❀❀❀

❀❀❀❀❀❀❀❀❀❀❀❀❀❀❀❀❀❀❀❀❀❀❀❀❀❀❀❀

And the manna was as coriander seed, and
the colour thereof as the colour of bdellium.

Numbers 11:7

GUMBO FILÉ

This is one of the classics of Creole cookery and is still to
be had in New Orleans in the right places.

Brown a tablespoon of lard in a casserole and add a chopped
onion. Cut up a chicken into small pieces and place them in
the lard. Keep stirring the chicken until it is almost done.
When well browned, cut up a slice of ham and add it to the
chicken. Cut up three pods of red pepper and add them as
well. Salt to taste. Add four cups of boiling water and let the
whole simmer for three hours. A half hour before it is to be
served, add three dozen oysters with their liquor. Just before
serving stir in half a tablespoon of filé powder.

❀❀❀❀❀❀❀❀❀❀❀❀❀❀❀❀❀❀❀❀❀❀❀❀❀❀❀❀

SPICE COOKERY

✿✿✿✿✿✿✿✿✿✿✿✿✿✿✿✿✿✿✿✿✿✿✿✿✿✿✿✿✿✿

He will kill a man for a mess of mustard.

Old English Proverb

APPLE BALLS

These make a pretty garnish for chicken or roasts. Make a syrup of three quarters of a cup of sugar, one cup of water, six cloves, a few red cinnamon candies, and the thin rind of half a lemon. Peel some apples and cut them into balls with a potato cutter. Boil your syrup for a few minutes, and then remove the cloves and the lemon rind. Drop in the apple balls and poach until they are transparent but take care that they do not lose their shape.

✿✿✿✿✿✿✿✿✿✿✿✿✿✿✿✿✿✿✿✿✿✿✿✿✿✿✿✿✿✿

❋❋❋❋❋❋❋❋❋❋❋❋❋❋❋❋❋❋❋❋❋❋❋❋❋❋❋❋❋❋

Marco Polo saw ginger growing in both China and India. And Sir John Mandeville, plagiarizing from some traveler to the East, wrote: "Be all that Contree growen the gode Gyngevere: and therefore thire gon the Marchauntes for Spicerye."

Vernon Quinn: Roots

FRUIT CAKE

I copied this amusing recipe from a child's book published some years ago, and it is much better than its rhyme.

Mos' eve'ything dat you kin bake you gotter put into fruit cake. One poun' uv flour en suguh each, six eggs (or seben ef dey's in reach), one half poun' uv currants picked, en same uv seede raisins nicked. One fo'th a poun' uv citron cut, one teaspoonful uv grated nut-meg, one uv cinnamon, en las' uv brandy jes one single glass. Cream buttuh'n suguh, add the yolks uv beaten eggs; en den mos' folks does alternate de whites en spice wid flour to make de cake look nice. Add fruit en brandy las' uv all, en den pray dat yo' cake 'ont fall.

❋❋❋❋❋❋❋❋❋❋❋❋❋❋❋❋❋❋❋❋❋❋❋❋❋❋❋❋❋

✳✳✳✳✳✳✳✳✳✳✳✳✳✳✳✳✳✳✳✳✳✳✳✳✳✳✳✳✳✳

30th July 1582. In Lisbon there has arrived a ship from India of the name of Buen Jesus. *She brings five thousand five hundred quintals of pepper, two thousand of cloves, much cinnamon and other spices.*

Fugger News Letters

BLACK WALNUT CAKE

Black walnuts are not everyone's meat, and some insist that it is an acquired taste. Here is a simple but excellent cake. Cream three quarters of a pound of butter with one pound of sugar. Add six eggs and mix well. Grate in one whole nutmeg and add one pound of sifted flour. Finally, add three quarters of a pound of black walnuts. Bake in a loaf pan.

✳✳✳✳✳✳✳✳✳✳✳✳✳✳✳✳✳✳✳✳✳✳✳✳✳✳✳✳✳✳

❋ ❋

*Beside that he had of the merchantmen, and
of the traffick of the spice merchants, and
of all the kings of Arabia, and of the gover-
nors of the country.*

I Kings 10:15

SPICED CANTALOUPE

Slice and pare ripe cantaloupes and place in a jar. Cover
with vinegar and let stand overnight. Pour off the vinegar and
to each quart add two and a half pounds of sugar, one tablespoon of whole cloves, two sticks of cinnamon and three
blades of mace. Put the vinegar on to boil with the spices and
then add the cantaloupe. When it is transparent remove the
fruit and continue boiling the syrup a little longer. Take fruit
and put it into jars and cover with boiling syrup.

❋ ❋

SPICE COOKERY

❀ ❀

The Greeks said: Owls to Athens,
Attica abounding with these birds...
the Orientals: Pepper to Hindostan.

Oxford Dictionary of English Proverbs

GINGERBREAD

Bring one cup of molasses and half a cup of butter to a boil.
Sift two and one-third cups of flour with a pinch of salt, one
and three-quarters teaspoon of soda, one teaspoon of ginger,
one teaspoon of cinnamon and one-quarter teaspoon of cloves.
Add one cup of sour milk to the molasses and butter and then
the spiced flour. Stir well and bake in a buttered shallow pan
for about forty minutes.

❀ ❀

❀❀❀❀❀❀❀❀❀❀❀❀❀❀❀❀❀❀❀❀❀❀❀❀❀❀❀❀

The world consumes more pepper than any other spice, the percentages being 55 for pepper and 45 for all the rest.

PUMPKIN PIE

To one and one half cups of cooked and strained pumpkin, add one cup of sugar (half white and half brown), half a teaspoon of cinnamon, quarter of a teaspoon of nutmeg. When thoroughly mixed, add two tablespoons of melted butter, the beaten yolks of three eggs, and one half cup of milk. Add a pinch of salt and beat well. Beat the three egg whites and fold them into the mixture. Pour into an unbaked shell and bake until firm. When cool, cover with whipped cream.

❀❀❀❀❀❀❀❀❀❀❀❀❀❀❀❀❀❀❀❀❀❀❀❀❀❀❀❀

� � � � � � � � � � � � � � � � � � � � � � � � � �des

Accustomed by their intercourse with the Orientals to the burning savour of spices, soon they were not able to get along without them. They could not prepare famous dishes without plentiful use of spice. Romancers of the era of the Crusades sang the praises, on nearly every page, of cinnamon, musk, clove, and ginger.

Historians' History of the World

CHICKEN CURRY

Cook, but do not brown, one onion and two cloves of garlic finely chopped together. To this add one tablespoon of ground coriander, one teaspoon of dry mustard, one teaspoon of ground cummin, one teaspoon of ground turmeric, one half teaspoon of ground ginger, one half teaspoon of ground chili pepper. Cut up a chicken and fry it in this mixture for about five minutes. Add thin cocoanut milk just sufficient to cover the chicken. Simmer gently until gravy begins to thicken and the chicken is tender. Then add a tablespoon of thick cocoanut milk. Salt to taste and a squeeze of lemon juice.

This is an authentic recipe of E. P. Veerasawmy.

� ✭

❋❋❋❋❋❋❋❋❋❋❋❋❋❋❋❋❋❋❋❋❋❋❋❋❋❋❋❋

Heap cassia, sandal-buds and stripes
Of albdanum, and aloe-balls.

Browning: Paracelsus

CABBAGE CURRY

Take a small cabbage and cut it into small pieces, soak in salted water for an hour, wash and dry in a cloth. Put it in a pan and cook it with two cups of brown stock until it is half done, in other words, for about fifteen minutes. Mix a pinch of saffron with a little water to a paste, add it to the cabbage together with two large spoons of chopped lean ham, one onion sliced thin, a pinch of salt, a generous pinch of cayenne. (This may make it too hot!) Mix thoroughly and simmer until the cabbage is tender. If it gets too dry while cooking, a little more stock or some milk may be added. Serve in a ring of rice.

❋❋❋❋❋❋❋❋❋❋❋❋❋❋❋❋❋❋❋❋❋❋❋❋❋❋❋❋

✾ ✾

The kingdom of heaven is like to a grain of mustard seed, which a man took, and sowed in his field.

St. Matthew 13:31

COURT BOUILLON

There are a number of recipes in which fish plays a prominent part that are called Court Bouillon. This is incorrect, for in France, where it originated, Court Bouillon is merely the broth in which the fish is cooked and it is, or should be, prepared with great care.

Mix your bouillon and let it boil for half an hour and it will be ready to receive your fish. If using it for crab, lobster, or shrimp, try letting the shellfish cool in the bouillon and notice the taste! To a half bottle of white wine, add some chopped parsley, a pinch of salt, a slice of lemon, two cloves or garlic, one chopped onion, two cloves, one stalk of celery, six pepper corns, one teaspoon of thyme, and two bay leaves. Add enough cold water to make sufficient liquid to cover the fish to be cooked in it.

✾ ✾

Pepper is blacke
And hath a good smacke
And euery man doth it bye.

John Heywood: Proverbs

RIZ À L'INDIENNE

This is an unusual method of preparing rice. Place one cup of rice in half a cup of melted butter and cook slowly, stirring all the while, until the rice is browned. Add another half cup of butter and one chopped onion. Crush six pepper corns and six cardamoms together with a little salt and add to the rice. Add a bay leaf, a little cinnamon, and a pinch of saffron dissolved in a little water. Put in half a cup of seeded raisins and half a cup of hot stock. Cover, and let it simmer slowly until the rice is tender. It must be watched carefully and more stock added from time to time if necessary. When finished, all of the liquid should be absorbed.

✿ ✿

What are little boys made of, made of?
What are little boys made of?
Snaps and snails, and puppy-dogs' tails;
And that's what little boys are made of,
*   made of.*
And what are little girls made of, made of,
*   made of?*
What are little girls made of?
Sugar and spice, and all that's nice;
And that's what little girls are made of,
*   made of.*

Nursery Rhymes collected by James
Orchard Halliwell.

MOLASSES SOUFFLÉ

Melt three tablespoons of butter and mix with four tablespoons of flour and three quarters of a cup of milk. Add a pinch of salt, half a cup of molasses, half a teaspoon of ginger and half a teaspoon of cinnamon. Beat the yolks of four eggs with three tablespoons of sugar and add to the mixture. When cool fold in the beaten whites of the four eggs and turn into a buttered baking dish. Sprinkle a little granulated sugar on top. Bake in a moderate oven for fifty minutes.

✿ ✿

✾ ✾

Fly like a youthful hart or roe
Over the hills where spices grow.

Isaac Watts: Hymns and Spiritual Songs

CHILI CON CARNE

Brown one chopped onion and two minced cloves of garlic in two tablespoons of lard or bacon drippings. Mix six table-spoons of chili powder with one tablespoon of flour and add to the fat. Take two pounds of beef and one pound of pork and either cut it into very small cubes or grind it and add. Over this rub one can of tomatoes through a sieve. Cover the pan and cook for half an hour. Add one tablespoon of salt and one tablespoon of orégano and simmer for two hours. This is served with a dish of red kidney beans on the side and one of boiled rice.

✾ ✾

SPICE COOKERY

❀ ❀

Spikenard and saffron, calamus and cinnamon with all trees of frankincense, myrrh and aloes, with all the chief spices.

Song of Solomon 4:14

CINNAMON TOAST

This perfect accompaniment for afternoon tea can be so good and rarely is. Take slices of bread, remove the crusts, and cut into strips. Toast one side to a light brown. Cream four tablespoons of butter and spread on the hot, untoasted side. Mix four tablespoons of powdered sugar with three of cinnamon and sprinkle over the buttered side. Put back in the oven until sugar is melted. Serve in a covered dish at once.

❀ ❀

❀❀❀❀❀❀❀❀❀❀❀❀❀❀❀❀❀❀❀❀❀❀❀❀❀❀❀❀

Better is one grain of hot pepper than a basketful of pumpkins. Just as a grain of pepper imparts more flavour than a heap of vegetables, so a little keen reasoning is worth more than a great deal of useless learning.

Oxford Dictionary of English Proverbs

HOW TO MAKE A POMANDER

Originally a pomander was a little case of silver made of several parts, which opened up and contained various aromatic scents. How the name was applied to the pomander described here is not known.

Take a small, thin-skinned orange and stick whole cloves into it until the surface is entirely studded. Roll the orange in powdered orris root and powdered cinnamon, patting on as much as you can. Wrap in tissue paper and put it away for several weeks. Remove and shake off the surplus powder and the pomander is ready for use. They can be hung up in closets by means of ribbon where they will retain their fragrance and aroma for years.

❀❀❀❀❀❀❀❀❀❀❀❀❀❀❀❀❀❀❀❀❀❀❀❀❀❀❀

SPICE COOKERY

✻✻✻✻✻✻✻✻✻✻✻✻✻✻✻✻✻✻✻✻✻✻✻✻✻✻✻✻✻✻

Nose, nose, nose, nose!
And who gave thee that jolly red nose?
Sinament and Ginger,.Nutmeg and Cloves,
And that gave me my jolly red nose.

Thomas Ravenscroft: Deuteromela

PEA SOUP

This is an excellent dish to make when you have a ham bone in the house. Soak two cups of split peas, yellow or green, in two cups of water over night. Next morning place them in a pot, add six more cups of water, two diced carrots, one bay leaf, an onion studded with four cloves, salt to taste and freshly ground black pepper. Cook slowly until the peas are soft. Remove the ham bone and scrape off any possible bits of meat that may be left on it. Mash the soup through a strainer. Cut little cubes of bread, dry them in the oven, and then fry them in a little butter turning them often so that they may be well coated. Serve these with your soup.

✻✻✻✻✻✻✻✻✻✻✻✻✻✻✻✻✻✻✻✻✻✻✻✻✻✻✻✻✻✻

The older ginger and cinnamon become,
the more pungent is their flavour.

Chinese Proverb

ARROZ CON POLLO

Cut up a chicken and brown it quickly in a casserole in a little olive oil. Add one chopped onion and one chopped clove of garlic. Next add four tomatoes, one sliced green pepper, a pinch of saffron dissolved in a little water, one bay leaf, three cloves, salt and pepper to taste. Cover with boiling water and cook until the chicken is tender. Wash one pound of Spanish rice and add it to the casserole and cook until done and all of the juice absorbed. Add one tablespoon of olive oil and a small can of pimientos, and serve.

✿✿✿✿✿✿✿✿✿✿✿✿✿✿✿✿✿✿✿✿✿✿✿✿✿✿✿✿✿

Allspice is indispensable in making mince-meat, into which it is accompanied by cinnamon and cloves.

CABBAGE IN WINE

Cut up a red cabbage as finely as you can, being sure to discard all of the stalks. Place in a pan and add one cup of red wine and one cup of white broth, chicken or veal. Salt and pepper to taste. Cut up two red apples with the skin, also very fine, and add to the cabbage. Cook until the cabbage is done, but not mushy. When ready to serve season with a little butter and grate a little nutmeg over the top.

✿✿✿✿✿✿✿✿✿✿✿✿✿✿✿✿✿✿✿✿✿✿✿✿✿✿✿✿✿

❋❋❋❋❋❋❋❋❋❋❋❋❋❋❋❋❋❋❋❋❋❋❋❋❋❋❋❋❋❋❋

...candied apple, quince, and plum, and
gourd;
With jellies smoother than the creamy curd,
And lucent syrops, tinct with cinnamon;
Manna and dates...and spiced dainties,
every one
From silken Samarcand to cedar'd Lebanon.

Keats: The Eve of St. Agnes

VEAL BIRDS

Take veal steaks cut half inch thick and cut into three inch squares. Pound the pieces as flat as you can. Place a piece of lean bacon on each, a half bay leaf, salt and pepper. Dust them with paprika after you have rolled them up and tied them with thread. Brown them in butter and then place them in a casserole. Add a little boiling water, cover them, and let them simmer for three quarters of an hour. Just before they are done, add half a cup of sour cream and a little more paprika.

❋❋❋❋❋❋❋❋❋❋❋❋❋❋❋❋❋❋❋❋❋❋❋❋❋❋❋❋❋❋❋

SPICE COOKERY

✺✺✺✺✺✺✺✺✺✺✺✺✺✺✺✺✺✺✺✺✺✺✺✺✺✺✺✺✺✺✺

Awake, O north wind; and come, thou
south; blow upon my garden, that the spices
thereof may flow out.

Song of Solomon 4:16

CAFÉ ROYALE

Make strong, hot coffee. Take one clove, a two inch piece of stick cinnamon, a small piece of orange peel and one of lemon, and a lump of sugar. Pour in one teaspoon of Martinique rum and one teaspoon of cognac. Place another lump of sugar in a silver spoon, put some of this prepared liquid over it and set it on fire, then lower it in to the rest. Add your piping hot coffee and serve. These proportions are for one cup.

✺✺✺✺✺✺✺✺✺✺✺✺✺✺✺✺✺✺✺✺✺✺✺✺✺✺✺✺✺✺

❋ ❋

*The world renowned liqueur, Kümmel, is
made from caraway seed.*

FIG PUDDING

Cream one cup of butter with two cups of sugar. Add three
eggs lightly beaten; then three cups of bread crumbs, two
cups of figs cut fine, one half cup of milk, half a teaspoon of
nutmeg and half a teaspoon of cinnamon and one tablespoon
of orange marmalade. Mix well and fill into a mold and steam
for three hours. Serve with a custard sauce flavored with
vanilla bean.

❋ ❋

✽ ✽

He nibbles salt and hoards ginger.

Chinese Proverb

PECAN AND RAISIN PIE

Cream a half cup of butter with one cup of sugar. Add the beaten yolks of two eggs and one tablespoon of flour and beat well. Add one tablespoon of vinegar, one teaspoon of nutmeg and one teaspoon of ground allspice. Fold in one half cup of chopped pecans and one half cup of chopped raisins. Beat the whites of two eggs stiff and fold in. Bake slowly in an uncooked pie shell. Top with whipped cream.

✽ ✽

✻ ✻

If you beat spice it will smell the sweeter.

Old English Proverb

TOMATO SOUP

Cook one can of tomatoes with two cups of water, four cloves, one onion, a teaspoon of sugar and a pinch of salt for half an hour. Make a roux of two tablespoons of butter and two of flour and moisten with some of the soup until smooth. Strain the soup and add a teaspoon of ground ginger and serve hot. Place a thin slice of lemon with a clove stuck through the center in each plate.

✻ ✻

SPICE COOKERY

❋❋❋❋❋❋❋❋❋❋❋❋❋❋❋❋❋❋❋❋❋❋❋❋❋❋❋❋

The grete galees of Venees and Florence
Be wel ladene wyth thynges of com-
placence,
All spicerye and other grocers ware,
Wuth swete wynes, all manere of chaffare.

The Libelle of Englyshe Polycy

SWEET POTATO PUFF

Boil six sweet potatoes in their skins. Peel and mash with half a cup of cream, salt, pepper, one tablespoon of brown sugar, one quarter teaspoon of nutmeg and the same of cloves. Beat them until light and place them in a shallow baking dish. Brush with melted butter and brown under the broiler flame.

❋❋❋❋❋❋❋❋❋❋❋❋❋❋❋❋❋❋❋❋❋❋❋❋❋❋❋❋

❋ ❋

"A loaf of bread," the Walrus said,
Is what we chiefly need:
Pepper and vinegar besides
Are very good indeed—
Now if you're ready, Oysters dear,
We can begin to feed."

Lewis Carroll: The Walrus and the
Carpenter

SPICED PRUNES

Wash one pound of prunes and soak over night. Put them on to boil in the water in which they were soaked. Tie three blades of mace, two teaspoons of whole cloves, three pepper corns and one teaspoon of whole allspice in a bag and cook them with the prunes. Simmer the prunes until tender, remove from the juice. Add one cup of sugar and a quarter of a cup of vinegar to the juice and boil for five minutes and pour over the prunes.

❋ ❋

SPICE COOKERY

✿✿✿✿✿✿✿✿✿✿✿✿✿✿✿✿✿✿✿✿✿✿✿✿✿✿✿✿✿✿

Woe unto you,...for ye pay tithe of mint
and anise and cummin.

Matthew 23:23

STEAMED SPICE PUDDING

Soak four cups of bread crumbs in one cup of milk and beat until smooth. Add half a cup of molasses, half a cup of melted butter, two teaspoons of cinnamon, one quarter teaspoon of cloves, one quarter teaspoon of allspice, and one teaspoon of soda. Chop one cup of seeded raisins and half a cup of finely chopped citron and mix the fruit with a little flour. Pour into a greased mold and steam for three hours. Serve with hard sauce sprinkled with cinnamon or a soft custard flavored with vanilla.

✿✿✿✿✿✿✿✿✿✿✿✿✿✿✿✿✿✿✿✿✿✿✿✿✿✿✿✿✿

❋ ❋

The short narcissus and fair daffodil,
Pansies to please the sight, and cassie sweet
to smell.

Dryden's Virgil

NUTMEG CREAM FROSTING

Combine one cup of sugar with half a cup of heavy sour cream and boil for one minute, stirring all the time. Remove from fire, add a quarter teaspoon of freshly grated nutmeg and beat until it becomes white and thick; this will take about fifteen minutes with an electric beater.

❋ ❋

SPICE COOKERY

❀❀❀❀❀❀❀❀❀❀❀❀❀❀❀❀❀❀❀❀❀❀❀❀❀❀❀

INDEX OF AUTHORS

Bible, The, 14, 24, 30, 31, 43, 66, 70, 75, 79, 85, 91
Browning, Robert, 74
Carroll, Lewis, 26, 90
Cervantes, 53
Chinese Proverbs, 82, 87
Concise Oxford Dictionary, 13
de Tèrey, Benno, 20
Dryden, John, 92
English Proverbs, 67, 71, 80, 88
Fugger News Letters, 69
Gilbert, William S., 29
Goldsmith, Oliver, 21
Gouffé, Jules, 28
Halliwell, James Orchard, 77
Hamilton, Thomas, 35
Herrick, Robert, 41
Heywood, John, 76
Hibben, Sheila, 37
Hippocrates, 65
Historians' History of the World, 73
Keats, John, 84
King, William, 17
Laverty, Maura, 15

Libelle of Englyshe Polycy, 89
Liber Cure Cocorum, 23
Mandeville, John, 33, 68
Milton, John, 64
Normand, Jacques, 56
Nursery Rhymes, 61, 77
Peck, Anne Merriman, 16
Publius Syrus, 34
Quinn, Vernon, 68
Ravenscroft, Thomas, 81
Ruskin, John, 54
Russell, John, 28
Shakespeare, 20, 25, 30, 48
Sowle, Henrietta ("Henriette"), 19
Squire of Low Degree, 63
Taylor, Mrs. Richards, 17
Veerasawmy, E. P., 73
Watts, Isaac, 78
Wells, Rhea, 13
Wheelwright, Edith, 59
White, Florence, 26, 58
Winslow, Thyra Samter, 35
Woodforde, James, 40
Wulf, Mrs. John, 18

❀❀❀❀❀❀❀❀❀❀❀❀❀❀❀❀❀❀❀❀❀❀❀❀❀❀❀

❋❋❋❋❋❋❋❋❋❋❋❋❋❋❋❋❋❋❋❋❋❋❋❋❋❋❋❋

INDEX OF RECIPES

Almond Soup, 58
Anis Plätzchen, 42
Aniseed Cakes, 64
Apple Balls, 67
— Sauce Cake, 43
Arroz con Pollo, 82
Baked Indian Pudding, 38
Barbecue Sauce, 50
Bermuda Turtle Soup, 29
Bishop, 14
Black Walnut Cake, 69
Boiled Spiced Tongue, 48
Bouillabaisse, La, 56
Brown Betty, 40
Cabbage Curry, 74
— in Wine, 83
Café Brûlot, 44
— Royale, 85
Cheese Spread, 54
Chicken Curry, 73
— — Soup, 47
Chili con Carne, 78
— Sauce, 52
Cinnamon Stars, 22
— Toast, 79

Court Bouillon, 75
Cumberland Sauce, 24
Curried Carrots, 49
— Eggs, 19
Curry Salad Dressing, 36
Fig Pudding, 86
Fruit Cake, 68
— Cookies, 39
Gazpacho, 37
Gingerbread, 71
Ginger Crisps, 23
— Cupcakes, 32
Green Tomato Chutney, 18
Gulyás, 20
Gumbo Filé, 66
Hippocras, 65
Lamb Chops Marinade, 63
Linzertorte, 15
Marrow Balls, 33
Meat Loaf, Company, 35
Mixed Spices, 28
Molasses Soufflé, 77
Mousaka, 59
Mulled Wine, 27
Mustard Sauce, 16

❋❋❋❋❋❋❋❋❋❋❋❋❋❋❋❋❋❋❋❋❋❋❋❋❋❋

SPICE COOKERY

✳✳✳✳✳✳✳✳✳✳✳✳✳✳✳✳✳✳✳✳✳✳✳✳✳✳✳✳✳✳

Nasturtium Seeds, 26
Nutmeg Cream Frosting, 92
Pea Soup, 81
Pecan and Raisin Pie, 87
Pfeffernüsse, 61
Philadelphia Pepper Pot, 34
Pickled Eggs, 45
Pomander, How to make a, 80
Poppy Seed Crescents, 41
Porcupines, 51
Pruneaux au Vin Rouge, 25
Prune Ice Cream, 31
Pumpkin Pie, 72
Riz à l'Indienne, 76
Saffron Rice, 53

Sauerbraten, 21
Scrambled Eggs à l'Indienne, 55
Scripture Cake, 30
Spice Cake, 60
— Pudding, Steamed, 91
Spiced Cantaloupe, 70
— Cherries, 46
— Prunes, 90
Sweet Potato Puff, 89
Székelygulyás, 57
Tomato Soup, 88
— — Cold, 13
Turkish Rice, 17
Veal Birds, 84
Wassail Bowl, 62

✳✳✳✳✳✳✳✳✳✳✳✳✳✳✳✳✳✳✳✳✳✳✳✳✳✳✳✳

CALVIN LEE'S

CHINESE COOKING

FOR AMERICAN KITCHENS

150 EASY RECIPES · FOOD AND CULTURE IN AMERICA
WHAT AND HOW TO BUY · SEASONING AND TEA CHARTS

COACHWHIP PUBLICATIONS
COACHWHIPBOOKS.COM

COACHWHIP PUBLICATIONS
COACHWHIPBOOKS.COM

Pennsylvania German Cookery

A REGIONAL COOKBOOK BY
ANN HARK & PRESTON A. BARBA

COACHWHIP PUBLICATIONS
COACHWHIPBOOKS.COM

COACHWHIP PUBLICATIONS
CoachwhipBooks.com

SPAGHETTI
DINNER

BY
GIUSEPPE
PREZZOLINI

COACHWHIP PUBLICATIONS
CoachwhipBooks.com

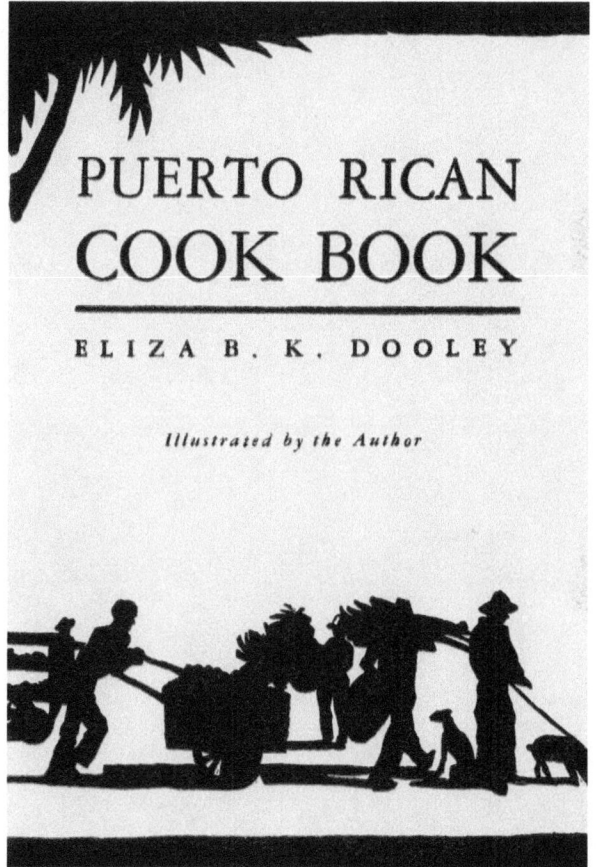